Why Are Scientists Turning to God?

Ralph O. Muncaster

D1568504

HARVEST HOUSE PUBLISHERS
Eugene, Oregon 97402

Cover by Terry Dugan Design, Minneapolis, Minnesota

By Ralph O. Muncaster

Are There Contradictions in the Bible?
Can Archaeology Prove the New Testament?
Can Archaeology Prove the Old Testament?
Can We Know for Certain We Are Going to Heaven?
Can You Trust the Bible?
Creation vs. Evolution
Creation vs. Evolution Video
Does Prayer Really Work?
Does the Bible Predict the Future?
How to Talk About Jesus with the Skeptics in Your Life
How Do We Know Jesus Is God?
Is the Bible Really a Message from God?
Science—Was the Bible Ahead of Its Time?
What Is the Proof for the Resurrection?
How Is Jesus Different from Other Religious Leaders?
What Is the Trinity?
What Really Happened Christmas Morning?
What Really Happens When You Die?
Why Are Scientists Turning to God?
Why Does God Allow Suffering?

WHY ARE SCIENTISTS TURNING TO GOD?
Copyright © 2002 by Ralph O. Muncaster
Published by Harvest House Publishers
Eugene, Oregon 97402

Library of Congress Cataloging-in-Publication Data

Muncaster, Ralph O.
    Why are scientists turning to God? / Ralph O. Muncaster.
        p. cm. — (Examine the evidence series)
    Includes bibliographical references (p.).
    ISBN 0-7369-0905-2
        1. Scientists—Religious life. 2. Religion and science. 3. Apologetics. I. Title

BV4596.S35 M86 2002
261.5'5—dc21   2001051854

02 03 04 05 06 07 08 09 10 / BP–GB / 10 9 8 7 6 5 4 3 2 1

Contents

Science and God—
Why Definition Is Important

The world has come to accept science for the basis of knowledge on virtually every subject. Why? Because the word "science" carries implications of extraordinarily precise experiments that define laws, such as physics, that we rely on daily. Building our homes and skyscrapers depends on such laws, as do machines such as automobiles, planes, and common appliances of refrigeration and heat. Science essentially "tells us what to trust, what to believe in."

Yet science has come to embody more than this factual "hard" knowledge, which is testable and can be proven to a high degree of statistical certainty. Today, "science" is often used for "soft" sciences, which can not be objectively measured or proven. Soft sciences include such disciplines as geology, anthropology, and basic biology. It would be nice if we could predict the finding of a gold mine or an oil field with the same precision as that of a solar eclipse, but we can't.

So we're faced with a dilemma. If we attach the label of science to views that support or dispute God, many people will blindly follow one or the other, *not* distinguishing between "hard" and "soft" science. In a sense, the word "science" has become our modern day "seal of approval" that something is true, without the need for checking out the facts behind the beliefs.

Unfortunately the line between hard science and soft science blurred over the past few centuries. This has created considerable misunderstanding among the general populous. In fact, the perception that "hard" scientists were turning away from a firm belief in God was incorrect. They weren't. The prominent advocates of soft sciences (Darwinian biology, some geology, anthropology) encouraged the perception that science generally discounted God.

Now the tide is turning. Recent discoveries and overwhelming evidence in the hard sciences is finally causing some of the world's greatest minds to counter many soft science theories.

The Key Issues

Authority of Science
(Claimed)

In recent years, the word "science" has been interpreted essentially the same as "authority." For example, people often claim "science has discovered_____" (you can fill in the blank). But has it really?

Intellectual honesty demands that we should really understand what the word "science" actually means. *Webster's* dictionary provides several definitions:

1. The *observation*, identification, description, *experimental* investigation, and *theoretical* explanation of *natural* phenomena.
2. Such activity restricted to a class of *natural* phenomena.
3. Such activity applied to *any class of phenomena*.
4. *Methodological activity*, discipline, or study.
5. An activity that appears to require *study and method*.
6. *Knowledge*, esp. that gained through experience.[1]

Note the enormous latitude given in the definitions! Science can also be—

- defined as either observational or experimental;
- described as "only natural" or any phenomena;
- classed as strictly theoretical or knowledge gained by methodological discipline and experience.

Is it any wonder that people are often confused when the tag "science" is applied to something that turns out to be incorrect? There are many examples throughout history where "soft" sciences proved to be in error (mostly observational sciences that didn't employ adequate statistical measurements). Many times, these incorrect soft science "theories" were eventually proven wrong by the hard sciences. For example, Copernicus observed that every day the sun rose in the east and set in the west. He concluded by observation theory (soft science), that the sun revolved around the earth. Centuries later, as the hard science of astronomy developed and statistical data about star and planetary motion were acquired, it was proven that the earth revolved around the sun.

This same type of thinking can be applied to the theory of naturalistic evolution that originated using soft science. Darwin's observations concluded that there was survival of the fittest among creatures—something few people debate today. Common body parts among animals were also observed. But without an understanding of the incredible complexity of life and the limits of the boundaries of time, Darwin postulated that favorable mutations would lead to increasingly favorable species. Soft science theorized a hard science conclusion that is now under significant attack because advanced technological tools have uncovered enormous information about the cosmos and microbiology that were certainly not dreamed of in Darwin's time.

The paradox is that a world that sees science as a single, complete system fails to realize that there are many subdefinitions within science. Some are "hard" and very reliable—for example, we all live our lives assuming gravity is real. We don't jump off cliffs. Unfortunately, soft science has achieved the same acceptance. How many of us would risk our family fortune based on a geological theory of gold underneath our home?

Science is not a catch-all phrase to the scientific community. They understand the difference between hard and soft science, which is now moving them closer to belief in God.

Authority of God
(Claimed)

In the not-so-distant past (before secularism took hold), the authority of God was prevalent. Approximately 80 percent of the world believed in some version of God.[2] For most of the world, the God of authority was the God of the Bible— recognized in varying degrees by Christians, Jews, and Muslims. In fact, of all people believing in a God, nearly 64 percent claim to fit into one of these faiths.[2] (While these three religions have very different concepts of God, they do recognize the God of creation as represented in the first five books of the Bible.)

As with the word "science," it's important to first define "God." For our purposes, we will not consider pantheistic gods. Instead, we'll go to *Webster's* dictionary to see what the commonly accepted definitions of God are:

1. A being conceived as the *perfect, omnipotent, omniscient originator* and *ruler* of the universe, the principal *object of faith and worship* in monotheistic religions.[1]

2. Other definitions of "god" (small "g") related to a "force," an "idol," etc.

The authority implied by this definition, both historically and now, is that this "God" is a) perfect, b) all-powerful, c) all-knowing, d) the originator of the universe, e) the ruler of the universe, and f) the principal object of faith and worship. The obvious difference between this definition of God and the general definition of science is the idea of naturalism versus supernaturalism. God is defined in a way that transcends naturalism. Science—except for the one "objective" definition (#3)—depends on naturalism. That one definition of science remains objective since it doesn't rule out scientific study in supernatural areas. It states that science includes indulging in *any class of phenomena* (that leads to knowledge). Thus, a study of science would also include a study of theology. Interestingly, that is precisely the way early scientists (those prior to the 1700s) viewed the discipline of science—an objective search for the truth *wherever it may lead.*

At first the idea of a supernatural God appears irreconcilable with the naturalistic view of science, which is commonplace today. As we will see they are not. It is the consistency of scientific knowledge and the evidence of God, seen in nature and the Bible, that is now turning many people back to God.

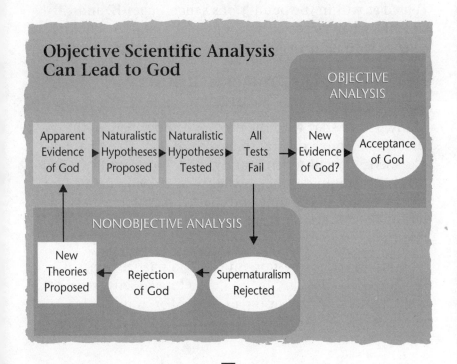

Objective Scientific Analysis Can Lead to God

OBJECTIVE ANALYSIS

Apparent Evidence of God ▶ Naturalistic Hypotheses Proposed ▶ Naturalistic Hypotheses Tested ▶ All Tests Fail ▶ New Evidence of God? ▶ Acceptance of God

NONOBJECTIVE ANALYSIS

New Theories Proposed ◀ Rejection of God ◀ Supernaturalism Rejected

The Key Issue of Science and God

As the majority of definitions for "science" indicate, it is usually associated with *naturalism*. Today, many people, including nonscientists, assume that everything that exists must have a natural explanation. Any suggestion of "miracle" or "supernatural" is considered impossible and absurd—therefore, "unscientific."

Hence, the idea of strict naturalism is associated in many people's minds with science. Throughout history this has not always been the case. The historical summary of the relationship of scientific thinking and God, reviewed on pages 10 through 23 indicate that there was a time when miracles, God, and supernatural events were widely accepted as within the bounds of science. Pages 12 and 13 describe what caused a shift in popular opinion equating science with naturalism.

The Problems of Strict Naturalism

Many people start with the presupposition that anything that is not from a natural source is not real. There has been a tendency to call supernatural events "unscientific." Obviously this eliminates the possibility of miracles defined by a God outside of the time and space dimension we live in. It also violates key tenets of good science—to be objective and to find the truth wherever it leads.

Not only is such a presupposition "bad science" since it prejudices conclusions, it also doesn't make sense regarding what we do know about the universe. For example, by virtue of our existence, which we know to be true, there has to be an explanation for our existence. The only reasonable explanation is that God created us. The argument would apply even if we assume an infinite universe, which we know now is not true. Yet it's especially provocative with what we know to be a *finite* universe. A finite universe implies that there had to be a beginning— a cause or a Creator. Interestingly, this admission of the supernatural, called the Cosmological Argument, has been discussed for centuries, at least back to the time of Plato.[3]

The Contradiction of Standards

Whenever strict naturalism is maintained with the presupposition that supernatural events are impossible, there is a dual set of standards. The scientific method calls for an objective evaluation of results of experiments. Often such experiments rely on empirical data that is evaluated based on predictability of outcomes. Usually this involves statistical analysis. If the issue of the supernatural is precluded entirely, then it removes the supernatural from the standard testing methods already used and accepted by good science. Such a contradiction of standards has been held by some people in the past few centuries.

As accumulation of data of an omnipotent Creator becomes more overwhelming, more scientists are considering consistent standards, and more scientists are considering God.

Is There Evidence that God Exists?

Once people accept that supernatural events are worthy of being evaluated with the same standards as natural events (just as scientists once did), it becomes easier to evaluate the existence and nature of God. Although the world has gone through a period from the early 1700s until the mid-1900s when it was deemed "unscientific" to attempt to seek "evidence" of God, in recent years even major universities are discussing scientific research grants to investigate God.[4]

Hard Evidence vs. Soft Evidence

As mentioned, the scientific world encompasses many definitions, and almost any area of study can be deemed "science" if the appropriate definition is applied. However, there is a difference regarding the type of support for the scientific study. Common terms used in the scientific community include "hard" evidence and "soft" evidence, which usually correspond to the definition of "hard" sciences and "soft" sciences.

Hard evidence is that which can be tested empirically. In other words, either by experimentation or statistics or both there is sound, quantifiable evidence of a conclusion. For example, laws of physics are arrived at through mathematical equations then tested by experimentation. The resultant laws of gravity, thermodynamics, and the like are extremely predictable. Bodies in motion, calculations of force, and solar eclipses are also verifiable. Physics is "hard" science.

As would be expected from the language, soft evidence theories are gained by observation and conjecture. That doesn't mean they are wrong, nor does it mean they are inferior. Many of our greatest breakthroughs in science started with soft evidence that later was turned into hard evidence through testing. For example, medicines, Teflon, and microwaves were all "stumbled upon" by soft evidence and now are important to our daily lives. Yet we still cannot predict the existence of a gold mine or oil field (geology = soft science) with the accuracy we can of an eclipse.

"Sciences" such as anthropology, some geology, and basic biology are "soft" relative to physics, statistics, and molecular biology. Hard science is very reliable; soft science involves educated guesses.

The Increasing Hard Evidence for God

A recent shift of thinking toward God has been caused by an increasing amount of hard evidence for the existence of God and the decreasing credibility of "soft" evidence for no God. In particular, with modern tools, scientists are discovering new evidence of divine planning, including:

1. a finely tuned universe perfectly suited for mankind (see p. 26),

2. the incredible design of cells and DNA structure (see pp. 28–31),

3. the statistical impossibility of naturalistic evolution (see pp. 32–35).

Long held soft-science beliefs in anthropology, biology, and geology that attempt to deny the existence of God are faltering, though they are still taught in many schools.

Scientific Thinking Before Darwin

God and Science
Were United

Before Darwin, the existence of God was essentially a nonissue. Yes, there were some detractors, but the majority of the scientific community generally accepted the presence of a Creator.

In the days before Darwin, there were no high-powered telescopes, space probes, electron microscopes, and other high-tech tools we have gained in the last 10 years. Science was "innocent." In this modern day, it's hard to imagine that knowledge such as the basics of germs and sterilization were not discovered until about the time of the Civil War— about the time of Darwin. So it's not surprising that the elite of the scientific community readily accepted the existence of God. All they had to do was notice the incredible intricacies of life. At that time, they noticed the miracle of birth, the complexity of a human eye, and the incredible beauty of a flower. To them, it was inconceivable that such developments came about by chance. It was inconceivable that God didn't exist.

There Was No Reasonable Alternative

While some theories had been proposed, none were popularized with "evidence" of a "non-God" until *On the Origin of the Species* was published in 1859. Hence most scientists conceded that some kind of God was necessary, and most accepted a creation-type God. Interestingly, Dr. Craig J. Hazen, associate professor at Biola University and an expert in the sociological impact of neo-Darwinism, indicated that in the United States, scientists originally treated

Darwin's work lightly. While Europe embraced it, public opinion became the driving force behind Darwinian (non-God) thinking.[5]

Darwin Introduced a "Sense" of Logic

It's in human nature to seek ways to explain the "unexplainable." So when Darwin introduced an idea that used many soft-science observations to explain why mankind could arise from a primitive species, he faced a world eager to accept it. Even Darwin's admitted possible faults of his theory have been "glossed over" by nontheists. In particular, Darwin stated that fossils would eventually prove or disprove his theory, but so far the fossil record supports theists. Darwin also asserted that gradual changes would be necessary for his theory to "work"; his theory has now been disproven by fossil records and microbiology.

It is very important to recognize the limitations of Charles Darwin's knowledge and experience. Many of these are ignored today when Darwinism is taught—*even though this knowledge is available today!*

1. Darwin had few fossils to examine.

2. Darwin had no idea of the complexity of a single cell.

3. Darwin had no idea of the complexity of DNA.

4. Darwin had no idea of the planet complexity required for man's survival.

5. Darwin didn't know the finite duration of the universe.

6. Darwin couldn't compute statistical evidence because he lacked these facts.

Scientists Supporting God (Pre-Darwin)

Most founders of modern science avidly supported God. Unfortunately, it's easy to ignore or forget the great minds that integrated God with science prior to Darwin. However, they were many and well esteemed, and included—

Leonardo da Vinci (1452–1519)—Da Vinci was regarded by many as the founder of modern science. While he may be best known for his superb paintings, da Vinci also was a great engineer and architect. His studies included physics, aeronautics, biology, and hydraulics. He was also a sincere believer in Jesus and the church, as powerfully indicated by his famous painting of the "Last Supper."

Johann Kepler (1571–1630)—Kepler is best known for his discovery of the laws of planetary motion. Although utilizing work by such people as Copernicus, Brahe, and Galileo, he went beyond their studies and developed disciplines of celestial mechanics. Kepler was a devout Christian and studied for two years at a seminary.

Francis Bacon (1561–1626)—Best known for his establishment of the "scientific method," which stressed hard data versus philosophy, Bacon was a devout believer of the Bible.

Blaise Pascal (1623–1662)—Pascal was clearly one of the greatest mathematicians ever. Not only did he lay the foundations for conical sections and differential calculus, but he applied his scientific skill in development of the barometer. He is regarded as one of the founders of hydrostatics. A deeply spiritual man, Pascal logically indicated that becoming a Christian was a win–win proposition.

Robert Boyle (1627–1691)—Credited as being the founder of modern chemistry, Boyle made many discoveries in chemistry and physics. During his lifetime he was considered by many to be the greatest physical scientist alive, yet Boyle was also a humble student of the Bible. Much of his time and money went to mission work.

Isaac Newton (1642–1727)—Perhaps the greatest physicist of all time, Newton established laws of motion and gravity and developed calculus as an integral branch of mathematics. He anticipated energy conservation, developed the particle theory of light, and designed the first reflecting telescope. Newton wrote much on biblical subjects, including strong papers that refuted atheism.

Carolus Linnaeus (1707–1778)—Linnaeus is well known for identifying species groups. His system is, in essence, still used today. Some people use this grouping as support for evolution; however, Linnaeus' original intent was to identify species "according to the kind" indicated in Genesis 1.[7]

Michael Faraday (1791–1867)—Faraday is acclaimed as one of the greatest physicists of all time. He discovered electromagnetic induction and defined the idea of magnetic lines of force. Among his many inventions was the generator. Several units of physics are named in his honor, yet Faraday was a humble believer in the Bible. He was confident that divine truth rested in both science and the Bible.

Samuel F. B. Morse (1791–1872)—The invention of the telegraph immortalized Morse in the annals of science. His first message was, "What hath God wrought!" This is actually a quote from the Bible (Numbers 23:23) and was indicative of Samuel Morse's desire to honor God in everything.

What Turned Thinking Away from God?

The public started turning away from God during the "period of enlightenment" of the 1700s. The movement started slowly at first, then it increased significantly in the mid 1800s. Why? There were three major movements that deemed God "unscientific."

Naturalistic Evolution

The book *On the Origin of Species* by Charles Darwin was a bombshell regarding people's opinion of God. The research contained in the book seemed to provide credibility that natural processes (evolution) could take the place of the account God provided in the Bible, found in the book of Genesis. Obviously, if life could be randomly generated and expanded randomly, there would be no need for a Creator-God.

Darwin's theory essentially split the world. On one side, people still believed the Bible to be the ultimate authority on world events, including creation. The other side questioned the reality of the biblical account. Darwin's treatise was regarded as "science" at the time. As decades passed, many were troubled by the apparent contradiction of these two views. Either God existed as Creator or He did not. Ideas that combined evolution and God were developed, but none were consistent with the Bible.

Many scientists turned away from God in a movement that started in Europe and advanced to the United States. Top scientists buckled under the peer pressure of Darwinian evolution supporters. However, this tendency was primarily in the soft sciences, not the hard sciences. Even so, when notable scientists started supporting evolution as "fact," the theory crept into textbooks and became required curriculum of public schools. People were ridiculed if they didn't accept the idea of evolution.

Darwin Expresses Weaknesses of His Theory

There are several ironies regarding Darwin's theory and today's scientific knowledge. First, Darwin acknowledged that his theory would not work if small, gradual changes were not possible.[6]

"Hard" Scientists Maintained Belief in God

It's important to explode the myth that all of science turned away from God during the period from Darwin to the present. While this may be true to an extent in the soft sciences (geology, anthropology, general biology), it is not true in the hard sciences (physics, applied mathematics, chemistry).[4,5]

In hard science, evidence of God has been readily available and measurable for centuries. Therefore, there was no tendency to back away from belief in God. In fact Darwinian evolution was initially ridiculed by the "hard science" community in the United States.

As tools become more sophisticated, general biology is becoming more of a hard science called microbiology. As the evidence mounts, many biologists and others are returning to a belief in a Creator-God.

Second, Darwin was troubled by the lack of transitional species in the fossil record. He maintained that an enormous number must exist.[8] Now, with millions of fossils to examine, we find none that fit Darwin's model.

Higher Criticism of the Bible

The 1800s introduced a new problem for those who believed in the Bible. In the early part of the century, questions started arising regarding the validity of the Bible itself. This reached a peak in the United States in the latter part of the century.

Supposed "scholars" raised many issues—some very detailed. (In the following examples I've included modern discoveries.)

1. Some critics said the race of Hittites never existed. Others said the Hittites could not have existed at the time of Abraham as indicated in Genesis. (Modern archaeology has unearthed entire cities of Hittites! There is a museum dedicated to Hittite artifacts, and people can even earn a Ph.D. in Hittite culture.)

2. Critics said that camels could not possibly have been domesticated at the time of Abraham (see Genesis 12:16). (Archaeology uncovered paintings of domestic camels at the temple of Hatshepsut, near Thebes, Egypt.)

3. Critics claimed that the strong doors indicated in the Bible for Lot (Genesis 19:9-10) were not based on the history of the time because cities (and homes) in the region were in a state of decline. (Archaeologists discovered such doors in the city of Kiriath Selpher in the same area.)

4. Critics claimed that it was too early in history for the development of the sophisticated laws indicated in the first five books of the Bible. (A black stele [monument] has been discovered that contained similar laws written prior to the time of Moses.)

Darwinism, combined with distrust of the Bible, turned public opinion away from God.

The Industrial Revolution

Progress. Who would think progress would turn people away from God? When we consider that naturalistic evolution allowed a reason to believe that God did not create, combined with higher criticism that undermined the authority of the Bible, it's not surprising that man began to think he was capable of anything as technology improved. In essence, the industrial revolution, with its rapid improvements in travel, communications, and computation, created an idea that man could understand everything and control everything. Man could become like God.

The good news is that the ever-increasing acquisition of knowledge is now pointing scientists back to God! Based on historical factors, eventually that belief will filter down to the schools and the general public.

The Changes . . .

General Public's Interest in God

Period of Enlightenment (Aristotle)

High

1. During the Enlightenment, people began to recognize the knowledge science was gaining.

2. Darwin shattered the need for God by proposing creation never happened.

3. The Wilberforce-Huxley debate pitted evolutionists against Christians. Science was too young to know the "facts" were wrong. It incorrectly assumed an infinite universe.

4. "Higher criticism" of the Bible cast doubt on its content. It was before the discoveries of modern archaeology.

5. The Industrial Revolution caused humans to be prideful of their achievements.

Medium

6. Einstein's General Relativity Theory created a scientific stir because it meant, essentially, that time, space, and matter had a beginning.

7. The Scopes Monkey Trial was another debate between evolutionists and Christians. Christians "lost" because science was still too young and Einstein's theory was yet to be proven.

8. Calculations by Hubble supported Einstein's theory, meaning there was a specific beginning.

9. The electron microscope allowed humans to discover the complexity of cells.

10. The Hubble Space Telescope and the COBE space probe, among other things, provided significant proof for Einstein's theory. Knowledgeable scientists leaned back toward God.

High

11. The mapping of the human genome further indicated the incredible complexity of the cell.

Pre-1700   **1700**

. . . in Public Opinion

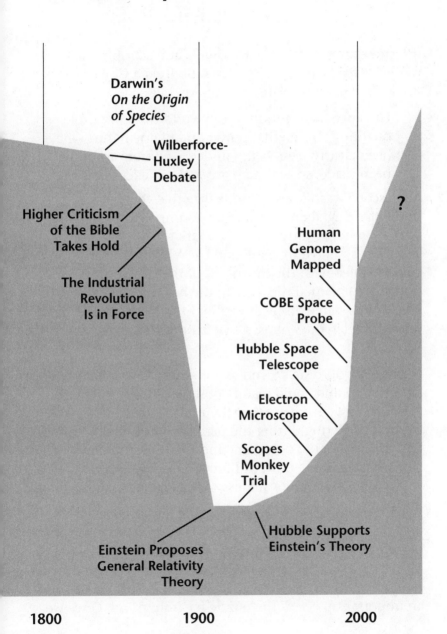

Darwin's
*On the Origin
of Species*

Wilberforce-
Huxley
Debate

Higher Criticism
of the Bible
Takes Hold

The Industrial
Revolution
Is in Force

Human
Genome
Mapped

COBE Space
Probe

Hubble Space
Telescope

Electron
Microscope

Scopes
Monkey
Trial

Einstein Proposes
General Relativity
Theory

Hubble Supports
Einstein's Theory

?

1800   1900   2000

Macro-Science Changes Minds

It's interesting that the astronomers and astrophysicists were the ones who consistently supported a God of the universe. Perhaps this relates to Romans 1:20:

> For since the creation of the world God's invisible qualities—his eternal power and divine nature—have been clearly seen, being understood from what has been made, so that men are without excuse.

A telescope wasn't needed to realize that there was something amazing about our universe. Long before telescopes, people used heavenly bodies to mark the days, seasons, and years just as stated in Genesis 1:14. While historians don't credit Galileo with the invention of the telescope, his version (1609) opened the door to the beginning of a long parade of incredible discoveries about the heavens. The most powerful telescopes on earth were built in the mid to late 1900s.

Because astrophysicists and astronomers have a hard science background and could readily observe a finely tuned universe, it's not surprising that their faith in God was relatively unwavering during the period of decline caused by Darwinism, Higher Criticism, and the Industrial Revolution. However, the more powerful tools introduced in the 1900s vastly increased our awareness of the evidence for God.

The Hubble Space Telescope, launched in April 1990, operates outside the atmosphere of the earth so it is capable of clearer, more distant images of the cosmos. In the early 1990s, data was being mapped that literally defined the edges of the universe by its background radiation. This was an important piece of the puzzle regarding God! Once we

knew the universe was finite, and we could estimate with accuracy the time since its origin, it necessitated a beginning and a beginner. It necessitated God.

The Hubble mapping was not the only basis for this conclusion. There was also the COBE Space Probe that was launched in 1989 and has traveled far into our solar system, providing vast amounts of data. Yet all this confirmation of the Genesis account of a beginning of the universe actually started with Albert Einstein's Theory of General Relativity, now proven by experimental physics. It was supported by Hubble's discoveries in 1929 regarding an expanding universe and discoveries by Arno Penzias in the 1960s. Even the enormous earth-based observatory "Keck (I and II)" in Hawaii, built in 1993 and 1996, add to the data and the understanding that the universe had a beginning—just as stated in Genesis 1:1.

Some may wonder why more attention hasn't been given to such great finds. Actually substantial attention was given. In 1992, Stephen Hawking, a renowned professor of mathematics, called the findings the "discovery of the century." George Smoot, project director for the COBE mission at Berkeley said, "It's like looking at God." Ted Koppel of ABC's "Nightline" even began an interview with some scientists on the matter by quoting the first two verses of Genesis.[9] Unfortunately, although physicists are very interested, most people still would rather spend time on more mundane issues.

The Anthropic Principle

All the macro tools available to us now are providing new insights into the intricateness of our planet Earth—and how it seems to be specifically designed for mankind. Again, we turn to hard science to see the evidence for this anthropic fact.

There was a time when science believed that only a few criteria were necessary for a livable habitat for humanity, including being a specific distance from the sun that would not be too hot nor too cold, having breathable air and residing on a planet that provides water. Obvious things were considered, but as scientists have become more involved in discovering what is really necessary for human beings to exist on earth, it is far more complex than originally believed. In fact, every year a dozen or more new criteria are discovered that are vital to human existence!

Things We Might Not Think About

There are more than 152 specific parameters that are crucial for life to exist on earth! Most of these are so finely balanced that even a deviation of a percentage point or so would be catastrophic. A few that are not readily apparent are reviewed below. (For a complete list, check out Reasons to Believe at www.Reasons.org.)

- *Global Distribution of Continents*—It is important that the distribution of land mass is greater in one hemisphere than the other. This allows even circulation of air, which provides a more temperate climate. Since water and land conduct heat at different rates, having different ratios allows for worldwide circulation, which keeps a thermal blanket over the earth.

- *Size of Moon*—The moon's size is ideal for a tidal force that circulates and "cleanses" waters of the oceans, but it is not so great that it causes catastrophes in shoreline cities.

- *A Single Moon*—Similar to the above problem, two moons would at times create tidal chaos when they came into alignment, causing unusually high tidal forces.

- *Tilt of Planet*—The tilt of the axis of earth is ideal for the development of seasons that provide for the maximum amount of life. If there was no tilt, temperatures would build to deadly extremes in more parts of the world.

- *Volcanic Activity*—Volcanic activity is important to the well-being of the planet because it spreads important minerals over vast distances, allowing improved production of crops.

While these are only a few of the 152 parameters, if all were tallied the probability of finding another planet like earth in the entire universe has been calculated to be one chance in 10^{-193}. Considering estimates of 10^{22} planets, this equates to less than one chance in a thousand, trillion, trillion, trillion, trillion, trillion, trillion, trillion, trillion, trillion, trillion, trillion, trillion, trillion, trillion.[10]

No wonder most astrophysicists have maintained a strong belief in God!

Micro-Science
Changes Minds

The most significant change in scientists turning to God is in the area of biology. Once biology was primarily a soft science based on observation. That is radically changing with new advances in microscopy, "wet" chemistry, and new tools such as Laser Tweezers. We can analyze the cell structure in ways that were impossible only a few years ago. Today, scientists have mapped the human genome (DNA structure) and will soon be mapping many other species. Biology is exploding with advances in tools and information.

Discoveries in microbiology are changing the minds of many biologists who are starting to recognize the extreme complexity of the living cell. They are also realizing the extensive complexity of naturalistic creation of the very first living cell, and the transition to more complex forms, which requires many transitions simultaneously.

One human DNA strand has 3.2 billion base pairs.

"Old" biology and modern microbiology have become a hotbed of conflict between those holding to the ancient Darwinian theories versus those proclaiming the contrasting technological advances that dispute Darwin's conclusions. Ironically, Darwin himself stated:

1. "Natural selection can act only by the preservation and accumulation of infinitesimally small inherited modifications, each profitable to the preserved being."[6]

   Science now *knows such changes were NOT infinitesimal—(e.g., the eye parts had to all work at once).*

2. "But, as by this theory innumerable transitional forms must have existed, why do we not find them embedded in countless numbers in the crust of the earth?"[11]

   Science has studied millions of fossils after Darwin, and it still lacks transitional species.

Anatomy of a Cell

Don't blame Darwin. He didn't have the tools and the knowledge we have today. As just pointed out, Darwin even acknowledged the weaknesses in his theory—weaknesses that are still perpetuated today. Unfortunately, much of the secular world has come to accept neo-Darwinism as scientific fact or as an excuse to reject God (i.e., no God was necessary for creation, therefore, no God exists). Modern science, in the area of microbiology, is presenting a very different picture for those willing to study it.

In Darwin's time cells were viewed as nothing more than "blobs of protoplasm." Today we know differently. A single cell, which typically is about one-thousandth the size of the period at the end of this sentence, performs all the functions of the most modern factory in the world.

Modern technology has enabled us to see into cell structures and understand them. Just a few of the many things a typical cell does (plant or animal) are listed below in a way that relates it to a factory. In truth, it is far more complex. A single cell:

1. generates power
2. manufactures a great quantity and variety of products
3. designates the function and relationship of these products
4. guides the final distribution of the products
5. packages certain molecules for distribution
6. manages transfer of information
7. assures quality beyond human capacity
8. disposes of waste
9. grows
10. reproduces

A human body has approximately 75 trillion cells that perform informational tasks that if written in books would fill the Grand Canyon 50 times every day. This is an example of the type of information recently learned that is turning biologists away from Darwin's theory. Cell biology includes:

DNA—The "central computer" that dictates all the actions of the cell. It contains 3.2 billion base pairs in one strand. If all the DNA were stretched out in a human body, it would extend beyond the solar system.

RNA—The "computer," similar to DNA, that transfers information to the "production floor" to create proteins.

Nucleus—The "control room" where DNA resides.

Ribosomes—The "production floor" where essential proteins are manufactured based on the RNA input.

Mitochondria—Energy "plants" based on respiration.

Lysosomes—Waste removal system.

Endoplasmic Reticulum—Transport network.

Golgi Apparatus—Packaging center for molecules.

Enzymes and Regulatory Proteins—Help the cell operate by speeding it up, slowing it down, or enabling or disabling specific genes.

Cytoskeleton—Amazing scaffolding of walls of the cells that adapt to needs.

Mathematical/Statistical Changes

The combination of the new knowledge about macro and micro changes in information have led to some very significant changes in belief in the existence of God by the scientific community involved in those disciplines.

A Creator-God

Once we accept the definition of God as the omnipotent Creator, as indicated in *Webster's* dictionary,[1] we must come to grips with the main issue: Did God create the heavens and the earth (as in Genesis 1:1), or did naturalistic evolution create the first life? Both cannot be correct.

In the time of Darwin, it may have been acceptable to assume that "stuff" (subatomic particles) came together to randomly form the first life. Then, according to Darwin's theory, favorable mutations allowed the survival of the fittest to proliferate, causing increasingly superior species. It all could seem logical. But now we know:

1. the universe is finite—be it 13 or 20 billion years old.
2. the vast complexity of DNA and cell structure.
3. the design built into the genes of creatures.
4. the mathematics of correct orientation of DNA/amino acids.

Scientists have far more information today than at the time of Darwin and through the last 100 years when God was "not necessary" according to the theory of evolution. Perhaps the easiest and most readily understood facet of microbiology is the issue of *chirality*—a point no microbiologist can legitimately explain today.

Chirality

Chirality is the necessity for DNA molecules to have connecting nucleotides in the "right handed" (dextroform) and the amino acids that are produced from RNA in the "left handed" (levoform). (Like magnetism, there need to be opposite "poles" to connect.) The next part of the problem is the minimum number of nucleotides necessary for the simplest bacterium (to start life) and the minimum number of amino acids needed to create the first protein. Microbiologists indicate at least 100,000 nucleotides would be necessary and 10,000 amino acid bonds. Fossil records fall far short of those numbers.

Accepting the fossil facts means the odds of evolution is the equivalent of 1,000,000,000 coin flips of "heads" in a row. All the nucleotides and amino acids would have to be correct to line up. One mistake would cause the entire chain to fail. The odds of having this random chance event of creating the first bacterium (again, far simpler than any that science has found) would be one chance in $10^{301,029,996}$. In other words, *it would be like winning 43 million state lotteries in a row with a single ticket for each!*

Chirality is a good indicator of God for molecular biologists because it's so simple . . . and so apparent.

Evolutionists Defend the Chirality Problem

After decades of study, no hard-science evidence has been produced to defend the chirality problem (and chirality is only one of many problems with evolutionary science). Since no hard evidence has been produced, a great deal of soft theories have come about. Theories of "optical purity" (the selection of correct chirality) are now moving to outer space for answers because none exist within naturalistic "earth means." These fanciful theories suppose amino acids and nucleotides were formed with correct orientation in outer space and traveled to earth. There is no solid experimental basis for such a theory. "Chaos Theory" is one such outer space idea. And dark holes are sometimes mentioned as a place for production of these particles that somehow came to earth at the right time to form the first living cell. Yet scientists espousing this idea fail to reveal that dark holes are far more destructive to life-origin cells than productive.

Any clear-thinking scientist might look into such theories, but he or she would certainly require significant testing before seriously advocating them. Unfortunately, the soft-science evolutionary community is sometimes more concerned with finding fantasy than fact, and often promotes such theories in a manner that makes them seem real.

Clear-Thinking Scientists

When scientists in applied mathematics consider the evidence and God, they come to the conclusion that God exists. The reasons are simple. As chirality alone indicates, it is virtually inconceivable that naturalistic evolution could possibly allow for first life to occur, let alone the vast development of species. Likewise, it is impossible to believe that a planet existed that fits humanity's needs so perfectly. These are obvious signs of a creator. Add to that the vast complexity of the human genome that has been recently mapped and the complex "factory-like" structure of a tiny cell, and there are substantial evidences of an omnipotent creator of the highest precision.

A cell 1,000th the size of the period at the end of this sentence is more complex than the most modern factory.

Why do some scientists still refute the idea of God, even with all this evidence? Many are simply refusing to accept the thought that God exists for reasons that are not very scientific. As stated earlier, there are many scientists who start with the unscientific *presumption* of naturalism, assuming anything supernatural is impossible. Others may fear a need to change their lifestyles to please a God. Still others make their livelihood trying to prove naturalistic evolution. There are many possible reasons, yet the scientific trend, particularly in microbiology, is a return to consideration of God.

Physicists Turning to God

Hugh Ross is an astrophysicist with a B.Sc. in physics from the University of British Columbia, a M.Sc. and Ph.D. in astronomy from the University of Toronto, and a research Fellow on quasars and galaxies as a post-doctoral student at California Institute of Technology. He turned to God when he noticed the precision of the universe and the accurate account of Genesis relative to science. Since then, he founded "Reasons to Believe," an outreach organization that has led many scientists to a belief in the Bible based on hard-evidence research.

In an interview on September 7, 2001, Ross explained how his education as an astrophysicist built his belief in God to the point that he was willing to help other scientists understand it. Through his ministry, which has spanned more than 15 years, he has explained in great detail how precisely the Bible meets the scientific record. This has caused many physicists and other scientists to reconsider biblical accounts and facts.

Ross, like Dr. Craig J. Hazen, indicates that in the "hard science" groups there has been no significant change over time in the acceptance of God. The "soft sciences" tend to be the areas that have dropped off because of Darwinian evolution theories, higher criticism, and the industrial revolution. Ross did indicate that many physicists, and especially microbiologists, are turning back to God based on new information from the recent discoveries of the mapping of microbiology.

One very interesting event that Hugh Ross discussed was a time during the cold war when he was invited to go to the former Soviet Union to speak. Expecting to speak on virtually any subject but God, he found overwhelming support to speak about science and God. After the lecture, one of the supreme delegates the front stood up and said, "You don't have to convince us about God. Seventy years of failure without Him has demonstrated He exists." At the end of the presentation, an invitation was given to accept Jesus as Lord, and people were encouraged to write down their decision for Christ. Since there was a shortage of paper in the Soviet Union at the time, pieces were being torn in two and passed out. At the end, hundreds of scientists of the Soviet Union accepted Jesus as Lord and Savior.

Many Esteemed Physicists Accept God

Dr. Boris P. Dotesenko, once a leader of nuclear physics, Institute of Physics, Kiev, USSR—After seeking asylum in Canada, Dr. Dotesenko determined that there must be a very powerful organizing force counteracting the disorganizing force (entropy) in nature. Some nonmaterial force needed to keep it controlled and organized. His final conclusion was that it had to be an omnipotent God. [12]

Patricia H. Reiff, professor of Space Physics and Astronomy at Rice University—Known for her work on the Apollo 14 mission, Reiff became an avid believer in God once she realized that God exists outside of the space–time domain. Speeds such as the speed of light didn't exist for an omnipotent God. Once such barriers were removed, Patricia was able to discover the reality of God in a way that is meaningful to an educated scientist. [13]

Dr. David Tonge, a native of Wales with a B.Sc. in mathematics (with first class honors), worked as an applied mathematician in a British Admiralty Electronics Laboratory and had experience in the Department of Mathematics and Computer Science in the Polytechnic of Wales. He was a leader in encoding and use of visual information supplied to the brain. Tonge received a Ph.D. at the University of London.

Dr. Tonge, like so many scientists, initially rejected the God of the Bible. His studies made him realize, however, the distinctiveness between the brain and the mind. The brain, he discovered, was strictly electrical, chemical, and structural. The mind, on the other hand, was based on thoughts, feelings, and will. While Dr. Tonge prided himself on answering all arguments on a naturalistic basis, he eventually recognized all arguments could not be defended as such. Supernaturalism and God became part of his thinking. In his quest for truth he studied the Bible, and his ultimate conclusion was that truth: ". . . transcends the logic of the scientist, the persuasive speeches of the politician, and the deepest reasoning of the atheist or agnostic philosopher."[14]

Dr. Randall J. Fisk, a Ph.D in High Energy Physics from the State University of New York, working later at the Fermi National Accelerator Laboratory (Fermilab), one of the largest particle accelerators in the world.

As a physicist, Dr. Fisk acknowledged the amazing simplicity and structure of the universe that caused even Einstein to acknowledge the essence of some form of "God." Dr. Fisk went further in his examination of the Scripture in discovering the many references to God being described in the cosmos, as in Psalm 19:1.

But, bottom line, it was his experience as a physicist that ultimately turned Fisk strongly into agreement with the God of the Bible. His experience with particle physics showed him that small particles (neutrinos) could literally pass through the entire earth undetected. Even today, it requires a three-hundred-ton "flash tube detector" to see them—and not all are being detected.[15] Fisk's reasoning was that there are some things God wants us to discover with our five senses, and other things he wants us to detect on faith. Ironically, new discoveries make it easier to accept God based on what we can detect, although not with the basic five senses.

J. Gary Eden, a scientist in Electrical and Computer Engineering at the University of Illinois, Urbana. Mr. Eden is quick to point out the observation by (perhaps) the greatest physicist of all time—Sir Isaac Newton—the "beautiful" system of the sun, stars, and solar system relative to the need for mankind to survive on earth.

Later scientists have called this unique design of the earth for man the "anthropic principle." Eden, as well as many other scientists, has observed the precise harmony required for life on earth. For it to exist elsewhere is beyond reason.[16]

Biologists Turning to God

Fazale R. Rana, Ph.D., was an agnostic/atheist having been raised by a semi-devout Muslim father and a non-practicing Catholic mother. Religion was not important in his home. In a sense, education was considered the "god" of the household. Dr. Rana rapidly progressed to a Ph.D. in chemistry at Ohio University and soon became a senior scientist with Procter & Gamble. In his initial years of higher education, Rana was very cynical of people who believed in God. That changed as his education grew.

During his graduate studies, Dr. Rana changed his thinking from a total exclusion of God to a belief in God. It happened through a series of studies that demonstrated to him the total impossibility of precise, multiple proteins produced in exactly the right way to create properly functioning cells of an organism. In a broader sense, it "told" him that random development of all the complexities of, for example, an eye, would be impossible without divine planning, as indicated in *Darwin's Black Box* by Michael Behe. His summary is that there has to be an intelligence behind the chemistry of the DNA that is converted to mechanical information as produced in the protein development in the cells.

The ultimate move to accepting God came, however, when he was challenged to read the Bible objectively, which appealed to Rana's pride as a scientist to seek the truth wherever it led.[17]

Professor Paul M. Anderson, professor in Biochemistry and Molecular Biology at the University of Minnesota, Duluth—Anderson outlined his initial struggles like many other highly educated people. His peers would argue that "science and faith are antithetical because religion 1) involves no experiments, 2) tests no hypotheses and 3) is committed beforehand to a set of beliefs."[18] Professor Anderson went beyond his peers to consider that none of these premises were convincing because the goal of science was to *determine truth* regardless of where it may lead.

For Anderson, the significant "test" involved no preconceived ideas because he admired former scientists who did not let prejudice influence current facts. As evidence mounted, Dr. Anderson embraced the idea of the God of the Christian Bible.

Professor John Patrick, professor of Clinical Nutrition and Biochemistry at Ottawa University—He discusses the probability theory of first life, and its impossibility. He reviews "coin flips" and the infeasibility of random life.[19] Most importantly, Professor Patrick reviews how God "fits" within the spectrum of good and evil. In essence, Professor Patrick concluded, "We are incapable of being responsible for the universe and, as creatures, we are not responsible for it."[20]

Robert Selvendran, Ph.D., a B.Sc. with honors in chemistry with pure mathematics as a secondary subject— Dr. Selvendran was awarded a research scholarship at Cambridge University, where he received his Ph.D. With more than 40 research papers published in scientific journals, he is highly regarded as an expert in plant biochemistry.[21] Born in a Hindu community, Selvendran experienced the thrill of discovering the Jesus Christ of the Bible.

Dr. Robert L. Herrmann, Ph.D. in biochemistry from Michigan State University, with postdoctoral research at the Massachusetts Institute of Technology. His expertise is in the cellular structure of aging. Herrmann responds to the primary causes of aging: 1) high caloric intake and 2) lack of exercise. He provides examples around the world that indicate these are aging issues. Furthermore, he divides aging cells from those that are more crucial (e.g., brain cells) versus ordinary cells (i.e., cells in the ordinary body), in the importance of life-sustaining growth. He claims both of these can affect the fundamental DNA structure in our somatic cells, causing aging.

Dr. Herrmann relates the aging process to people who sometimes have a "panicky desperation" to avoid aging and death. He relates this to the "unfaith" of some of his colleagues. Herrmann, himself, does not consider death as the end because of his unwavering faith in Jesus Christ as indicated in the Bible. He relates the life God has given him as infinite instead of the temporal, aging life so many seem to assume in his profession.[22]

Dr. C. Everett Koop, former U.S. Surgeon General—Dr. Koop has achieved numerous awards and honors that led to his position as the U.S. Surgeon General. He has served as president of the surgical section of the American Academy of Pediatric Surgery and of the American Pediatric Surgical Association. A Fellow of the American College of Surgeons and the American Academy of Pediatrics, Dr. Koop has memberships in many medical societies throughout the world. He has been a professor at the University of Pennsylvania School of Medicine, and has received honorary degrees in 5 institutions. He currently is the Elizabeth DeCamp McInerny professor at Dartmouth. Koop's credentials in the medical community are exemplary.

One might think such an accomplished pioneer in the medical community would feel human beings are able to "replace" God . . . or that God doesn't exist. Nothing could be further from the truth. Dr. Koop says, "The hallmark of my existence is the integration of my surgical life with my Christian Faith."[23] He further adds, "If I didn't believe that I had a God who was solid and dependable, a God who makes no mistakes, I couldn't continue what I'm doing."[24]

Universities Consider Intelligent Design

Dr. Ross indicated that several major universities are considering applying for research grants to fund studies on the probability of intelligent design (implying research regarding evidence of God).

Fueling this interest is the evidence of design in molecular biology coming to the fore, along with the now widely recognized anthropic principle (see p. 26), which indicates how finely tuned our universe is for human beings. Among the universities considering such grants are the University of Colorado, the University of New Mexico, and the University of California at Los Angeles.

Common Questions

1. Wouldn't a loving God allow good people into heaven?

Many people believe that living a good life and being kind to others is the way to heaven. Naturally, they are thinking of a "good" life in terms of our distorted human view; and such a life is far from God's standard. The Bible says that the *only* way to God the Father in heaven is through Jesus Christ (John 14:6). So will loving and "good" people who don't accept Jesus go to hell? Yes—but how can they be truly good if they reject the love of God's Son, Jesus, who died for them?

God will allow perfectly good people into heaven. But His standard of goodness is the perfection of His Son Jesus. Hence, there is simply no other way to come to Him except through Jesus—let alone the fact that every sin of mind or body we commit removes us further from Jesus' perfection (Matthew 5:28,29; Romans 3:22,23).

Everyone is imperfect, but the good news is that God has provided Jesus as a perfect sacrifice for us. He is our way to heaven. Not accepting God's gift of love and forgiveness through Jesus, despite the Holy Spirit's prompting, is unforgivable (Mark 3:29).

2. How can we ensure the right relationship to go to heaven?

When Jesus said that not all who use His name will enter heaven (see Matthew 7:21-23), He was referring to people who think using Christ's name along with rules and rituals is the key. A *relationship* with God is not based on rituals or rules. It's based on grace, forgiveness, and right standing with Him.

3. What do I need to do to have a personal relationship with God?

a. *Believe that God exists* and that He came to earth in the human form of Jesus Christ (see John 3:16; Romans 10:9).

b. *Accept God's free forgiveness* of sins and gift of new life through the death and resurrection of Jesus Christ (see Ephesians 2:8-10; 1:7-8).

c. *Switch to God's plan for your life* (see 1 Peter 1:21-23; Ephesians 2:1-7).

d. *Expressly make Jesus Christ the Director* of your life (see Matthew 7:21-27; 1 John 4:15).

Prayer for Eternal Life with God

Dear God, I believe You sent Your Son, Jesus, to die for my sins so I can be forgiven. I'm sorry for my sins, and I want to live the rest of my life the way You want me to. Please put Your Spirit into my life to direct me. Amen.

People who sincerely take the above steps become members of God's family of believers. New freedom and strength are available through prayer and obedience to God's will. Your new relationship can be strengthened by:

- Finding a *Bible-based church* you like and attending regularly.

- Setting aside time each day to *pray and read the Bible.*

- *Locating other Christians to spend time with* on a regular basis.

God's Promises to Believers
For today
Seek first his kingdom and his righteousness, and all these things [e.g., things that satisfy all your needs] will be given to you as well (Matthew 6:33).

For eternity
Whoever believes in the Son has eternal life, but whoever rejects the Son will not see life, for God's wrath remains on him (John 3:36).

Once we develop an eternal perspective, even the greatest problems on earth fade in significance.

Notes

1. *Webster's II New Riverside University Dictionary* (Boston, MA: The Riverside Publishing Company), 1984.

2. *Almanac of the Christian World* (Wheaton, IL: Tyndale Publishing, Inc., 1994), p. 80.

3. Hazen, Craig J., Philosophia Christi (La Mirada, CA: Evangelical Philosophical Society), 1999.

4. Ross, Hugh, Ph.D, interview September 7, Reasons to Believe, Pasadena, CA, 2001.

5. Hazen, Craig J., Ph.D, interview August 29, Biola University, La Mirada, CA, 2001.

6. Darwin, Charles, *On the Origin of Species* (Cambridge, MA: Harvard University Press, 1964), p. 95.

7. Morris, Henry, *Men of Science, Men of God* (Green Forest, AR: Master Books, Inc., 1988), p. 27.

8. Darwin, *Origin of Species*, p. 280.

9. Ross, Hugh, *The Creator and the Cosmos* (Colorado Springs, CO: NavPress, 2001), p. 32.

10. Adapted from ibid., p. 198.

11. Darwin, *Origin of Species*, p. 172.

12. Barrett, Eric C., and Fisher, David, *Scientists Who Believe* (Chicago: Moody Press, 1984), p. 1.

13. Anderson, Paul M., editor, *Professors Who Believe* (Downers Grove, IL: InterVarsity Press, 1998), p. 55.

14. Barrett and Fisher, *Scientists Who Believe,* p. 82

15. Ibid., p. 89.

16. Anderson, *Professors Who Believe*, p. 77

17. Rana, Fazale R., Ph.D., interview September 7, Reasons to Believe, Pasadena, CA, 2001.

18. Anderson, *Professors Who Believe*, p. 16.

19. Ibid., p. 30

20. Ibid., p. 31

21. Barrett and Fisher, *Scientists Who Believe*, p. 20.

22. Ibid., p. 164.

23. Ibid., p. 159.

24. Ibid., p. 152.

Bibliography

Alcamo, Edward I., Ph.D. *Theories and Problems of Microbiology*. New York: McGraw Hill, 1998.

Behe, Michael J. *Darwin's Black Box*. New York: The Free Press, 1996.

Dembski, William A. *Intelligent Design*. Downers Grove, IL: InterVarsity Press, 1999.

Life Application Bible. Wheaton, IL: Tyndale House Publishers, 1991.

Spetner, Lee M., Ph.D. *Not by Chance*. Brooklyn, NY: The Judaica Press, Inc., 1998.

Toumey, Christopher P. *God's Own Scientists*. New Brunswick, NJ: Rutgers University Press, 1994.